D1285230

Pebble™ Plus

Keeping Healthy

Taking Care of My Hair

by Terri DeGezelle

Consulting Editor: Gail Saunders-Smith, PhD

Consultant: Amy Grimm, MPH
Program Director, National Center for Health Education
New York, New York

Capstone press

Mankato, Minnesota

Pebble Plus is published by Capstone Press,
151 Good Counsel Drive, P.O. Box 669, Mankato, Minnesota 56002.
www.capstonepress.com

1 2 3 4 5 6 10 09 08 07 06 05

Library of Congress Cataloging-in-Publication Data
DeGezelle, Terri, 1955–
    Taking care of my hair / by Terri DeGezelle.
    p. cm.—(Pebble plus. Keeping healthy)
    Includes bibliographical references and index.
    ISBN 0-7368-4261-6 (hardcover)
    1. Hair—Care and hygiene—Juvenile literature. I. Title. II. Series.
RL91.D43 2006
646.7'24--dc22   2004026747

Summary: Simple text and photographs present ways to take care of your hair.

Editorial Credits
Sarah L. Schuette, editor; Jennifer Bergstrom, designer; Stacy Foster, photo resource coordinator

Photo Credits
Capstone Press/Karen Dubke, all

The author dedicates this book to Natalie DeGezelle.

Note to Parents and Teachers

The Keeping Healthy set supports science standards related to physical health and life skills for personal health. This book describes and illustrates how to take care of your hair. The images support early readers in understanding the text. The repetition of words and phrases helps early readers learn new words. This book also introduces early readers to subject-specific vocabulary words, which are defined in the Glossary section. Early readers may need assistance to read some words and to use the Table of Contents, Glossary, Read More, Internet Sites, and Index sections of the book.

Table of Contents

My Amazing Hair

Hair grows all over my body.

I have hair on my head,

face, arms, hands, and legs.

Hair grows from
under my skin.
Hair is made of keratin.

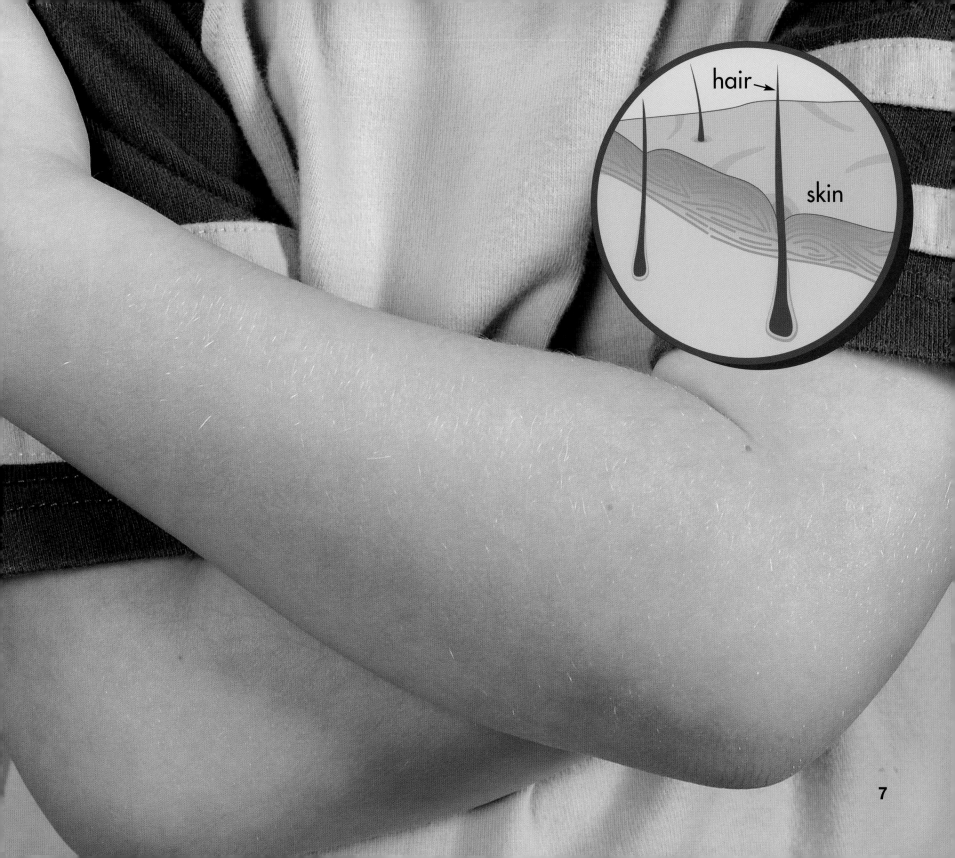

hair →

skin

I have more than
100,000 hairs
on my head.

Hair can be curly or straight.

It can be different colors.

I can wear my hair
long or short.
I get haircuts
to keep it healthy.

Clean Hair

I wash my hair
with shampoo and water.
I dry my hair.

15

I comb or brush
my hair every day.
I never share
my combs or brushes.

I get my hair checked
for head lice.
I use shampoo with medicine
if I have head lice.

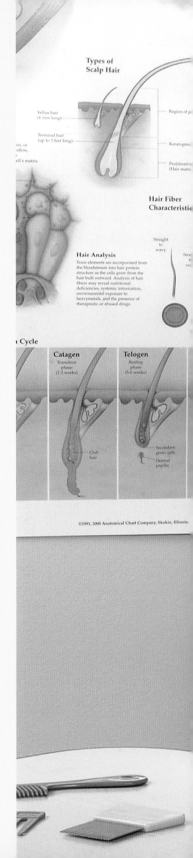

19

Healthy Hair

I feel good when
I take care of my hair.

Glossary

head lice—small insects without wings that live on people or animals; people can buy shampoo with medicine in it that kills head lice.

keratin—the substance that makes up a person's hair, fingernails, and toenails

shampoo—a soapy liquid used for washing hair; many people also use conditioner after washing their hair to make it soft and shiny.

skin—the outer covering of tissue on a person's body; skin is the body's biggest organ.

Read More

Derkazarian, Susan. *You Have Head Lice!* Rookie Read-About Health. New York: Children's Press, 2005.

Royston, Angela. *Healthy Hair.* Look After Yourself. Chicago: Heinemann Library, 2003.

Schaefer, Lola M. *Hair.* It's My Body. Chicago: Heinemann, 2003.

Internet Sites

FactHound offers a safe, fun way to find Internet sites related to this book. All of the sites on FactHound have been researched by our staff.

Here's how:

1. Visit *www.facthound.com*

2. Type in this special code **0736842616** for age-appropriate sites. Or enter a search word related to this book for a more general search.

3. Click on the **Fetch It** button.

FactHound will fetch the best sites for you!

Index

Word Count: 118
Grade: 1
Early-Intervention Level: 16